MW01484402

WHO WAS I SUPPOSED TO ASK?

LIVING IN GOD'S AUTHORITY

GLORIA D. JONES, PHD

BALBOA
PRESS

A DIVISION OF HAY HOUSE

Copyright © 2011 Gloria D. Jones, PhD

All rights reserved. No part of this book may be used or reproduced by any means, graphic, electronic, or mechanical, including photocopying, recording, taping or by any information storage retrieval system without the written permission of the publisher except in the case of brief quotations embodied in critical articles and reviews.

Balboa Press books may be ordered through booksellers or by contacting:

Balboa Press
A Division of Hay House
1663 Liberty Drive
Bloomington, IN 47403
www.balboapress.com
1-(877) 407-4847

Because of the dynamic nature of the Internet, any web addresses or links contained in this book may have changed since publication and may no longer be valid. The views expressed in this work are solely those of the author and do not necessarily reflect the views of the publisher, and the publisher hereby disclaims any responsibility for them.

The author of this book does not dispense medical advice or prescribe the use of any technique as a form of treatment for physical, emotional, or medical problems without the advice of a physician, either directly or indirectly. The intent of the author is only to offer information of a general nature to help you in your quest for emotional and spiritual well-being. In the event you use any of the information in this book for yourself, which is your constitutional right, the author and the publisher assume no responsibility for your actions.

Any people depicted in stock imagery provided by Thinkstock are models, and such images are being used for illustrative purposes only.
Certain stock imagery © Thinkstock.

ISBN: 978-1-4525-3645-3 (e)
ISBN: 978-1-4525-3644-6 (sc)

Printed in the United States of America

Balboa Press rev. date: 7/14/2011

I have written this book from the seat of imperfection and have dedicated it to those who share this seat with me. For those of you who have reached perfection and have learned it all that you need to know-put it down-this book will prove to be extremely boring for you.

My family knows that they have been the motivation for all that I have accomplished; I thank them for their love and support.

This book is dedicated to those like me who need just a little more instruction than what is given in traditional religious settings. If you have been sitting on the pews for years following traditions and maintaining appropriate behaviors (you know when to stand sit and sing in the service) this book is for you-let's move to the next level. We can live in God's Authority-for it is our God given right. Now we must learn how to exercise it.

CONTENTS

I
YOU DON'T KNOW WHAT YOU DON'T KNOW
(Proverbs 3:1-7)

I have spent the majority of my life working with two types of people-those who know what they know and those who don't know what they don't know. In the settings that I have been exposed, most of the people I have worked with, really don't know what they don't know. These are not untrained or unintelligent people, but are people who simply lack understanding of the continuum of knowledge and believe that their perceptions and experiences are the extent of or end of that knowledge.

I have been fortunate in my work to be required to understand that my perspective of a matter is most often irrelevant when working with people who are trying to make changes in their lives. Because they often believe that the choices they are making are good choices, based on what I perceive to be, their life experience to that point. My first understanding of this occurred when my son was about 4 or 5 years old. I was a single mom, living in Phoenix Arizona. I was playing softball on a team and during the game; my son fell off the bleachers. As you may know, a mother knows the cry of her child, I ran off the field (center field), and ran to the hospital with him in my arms. (Don't be impressed, the field sat behind the hospital on the base). He was screaming at the top of his voice, I too had joined him because as we were running through the field, frogs were jumping up around me. By the time we arrived at the reception desk; we were both screaming and crying.

Once the nurse realized I was not hurt, she attended to my son, only to discover that the injury was minor, he was just scared. I looked at him and told him "Hush, it's not that bad." He looked up at me with those beautiful brown eyes and said "But it is to me!" That was the last time that I looked at a situation only from my perspective.

As I worked with various families who were dealing with a multitude of problems and my church families over the years, I have come to realize that the enemy has maintained his deceptive campaign very well.

The current teachings of many of the churches are superficial and often not grounded in biblical principles. Many churches function from a place of tradition and rituals. Jesus himself warns us of these traditions when he scolds the scribes and Pharisees who were challenging the behaviors of the disciples in Mathew 15:1 calling them hypocrites because they focused on certain behaviors as more righteous than others yet none of these traditions would lead to salvation.

Having been raised in the Episcopal Church and exposed to the AME church, I understand when to stand, to sit, to kneel and to pray. I was completely unprepared for the Baptist Church and Pentecostal Churches. As my husband advanced in his growth toward Christ, I was expected to accompany him on this journey. While ministers spoke about the need for a personal relationship with Christ, readiness for roles in leadership in the church setting was unaddressed, particularly for the wife. I was fortunate in that an elderly woman in the church began to instruct me on the traditions of the church and my role as the wife of a church leader, however, not much of these traditions were grounded in the word. Now let me share with you, that following rules for the sake of following rules, is my major shortcoming. I have many, but this one has caused me more challenges. Regardless of my life situation, I have always read the Bible for guidance and direction. I believe that God has always provided me with direction, even when I wasn't ready to follow it. So I have always been challenged by seeking that justification or "permission" from man and have been surprised by the number of individuals who feel they were obligated to speak into my life, particularly from a place of authority. Thus the birth of the title, when God ordains you to a mission "Who are you supposed to ask?

As I asked myself this question over and over, I realized most people who asked this question really didn't know what they didn't know. When you don't understand the power of God, and how the Holy Spirit moves in a believer's life on a daily basis -you may feel the need to interject your approval or disapproval into the lives of others. As I have grown spiritually and experienced God for myself, I am less drawn to sharing my opinions about what God has called others to do. Quite frankly, it is none of my business. Many of you may find it difficult not to solicit validation from others when the Holy Spirit has spoken into your life. Their understanding of it does not validate it-your obedience to The Word does. Before I could truly encompass this basic principle of faith I had to first acknowledge what I did and didn't know and then embrace the desire to be taught. There are no age or education limitations which would prohibit you from having the need to learn. As you grow in the knowledge of God, you gain understanding and are blessed with His Wisdom. Therefore, the question is- *"Who are you supposed to ask?*

II
IT PAYS TO UNDERSTAND
(1 Chronicles 28:9-11; John 5:39-48; Isaiah 55:8)

Your value comes from understanding what your life's purpose is but also how it is connected to your family system. Values are based on what you believe. Moreover, what you believe provides vital understanding to the nature of your passion. Oftentimes your work is a continuation of another's and a link to the future. This was evident as King Solomon was selected to complete the dream of his father, David, through the ordination by God (1 Kings 2:1-4) to complete the temple. Sometimes these linkages occur and you are not even aware of the groundwork that has gone on, before you recognize the mission God has equipped you for in your life.

Since I was a very young child, I have been one that others' could come to for advice. If you had asked me at an early age what I wanted to be when I grew up, my first answer would have been a banker. I grew up in Columbus Ohio; they had the most marvelous banks. I just knew that you had to be important to work in such an establishment. I also felt that it was a place to help people; more often than not when my mom went into the back she came out smiling. So at the early age of twelve, I put on my Sunday best and took the bus across town to let the president of the bank know that I was available for work. I don't remember the gentlemen but he had a kind spirit, he "interviewed me" but told me the only barrier I had to employment was my age but if I still wanted to work at the bank when I turned 15, to come back and see him. This was the first lesson I had on how to treat "the lesser of God's flock".

It wasn't until several weeks later that my mother even realized that I had been there for an interview and the results (which were summarized in a letter from the bank). At about age 15 I decided that I wanted to be an attorney. I felt that in order for things to change-advocates needed to be developed to assist in this process. However, during my 9th grade a guidance counselor informed me that was a silly idea because I was colored (we hadn't quite adopted black or African-American) and I was a woman. I didn't argue with her but her rationale was quite puzzling to me because all of my life I had been told that "I can do all things through Christ which strengthen me" (Phil 4:8) and there were no color or gender qualifications in the Word.

Following a colorful high school experience, I graduated and attended college, pledging that I would do anything but work with alcoholics. My father was a recovering alcoholic and I often attended meetings with him and heard the many stories of the costs of alcohol on the lives on his group members. I also had firsthand experience with my own group of friends who thought drinking to the point of oblivion was "fun". Besides not liking the smell of alcohol, vomiting has never been a positive past time for me. I also realized at an early age that I had an extremely high tolerance for alcohol, so much so, that when I did engage in reckless drinking, I normally out drank whoever I was without negative side effects. I believe it was the Holy Spirit that first made me question how 105 lb woman could out drink any man she met and perhaps this was not a positive attribute. So I limited my drinking experiences to wine (believing it was less harmful than other drinks-remember I hadn't had any training yet) and began experimenting with marijuana. As I pursued my education, I was drawn to the field of psychology. I still didn't want to work with "those people" because I felt so much of the behaviors that I had seen were choices and quite frankly I was very judgmental of that lifestyle. If I could just stop-so could you, Even after completing my Masters degree, I had very little understanding of tolerance and addiction.

It wasn't until my own household was hit by the consequences of chronic alcohol and drug abuse did I begin to gain an understanding into this disease and into my calling. A daughter became addicted to drugs and my husband and I were called in to assist with her minor children. As it turned out, we raise all three to adulthood. During the early part of her addiction, I began searching what little research there was to find out what could drive such a wedge in someone's family. The understanding that I gained during that search resulted in the mental health and substance abuse treatment programs that I direct and manage unto this day.

It was over a period of 15 years after opening my first program that I met a woman from my hometown who told me that my father had been on the planning board for a residential treatment program for women and their children prior to his death in 1975. I had no earthly idea that he had even started this journey, or that I would bring his dream to fruition in Georgia. I have been blessed to see this process proceed through the next generations as some of my children have gained the necessary credentials to carry the work on. I learned early from my Grandmother that your life was God's gift to you; what you do with it is your gift to Him. What does your present look like? Because it pays to understand.

III
WHAT IS THE POWER OF YOUR SOURCE
(Acts 1:8; John 15: 6-7)

It is imperative to understand the "power" that drives you to do what you do as it relates to your life's purpose. Divine guidance not only provides direction but it provides the authority by which you complete your life's purpose. One of the most difficult concepts for Christians to grasp is that everything that they do is accomplished by the power that is endowed to them by God. This lack of understanding is based on the misconceptions we carry regarding submission and humility. This book focuses a lot on these two characteristics of the Christian believer. The human applications of these two characteristics are often attributed to weakness and powerlessness.

Our society boosts winning, overtaking, conquering etc. God's application of these characteristics is based in the love that you possess for Him. Jesus, however showed the ultimate demonstration of His love when He willingly suffered the unmerited persecution and subsequent death on the cross because of His obedience and love for the Father, "not my will, but yours". Our purpose is predestined, God says "I knew you while you were yet in your mother's womb and I know the work I have for you."

Our challenge is connecting to our power source and manifesting that power in our mission work. Most individuals that I have met who are on their true path, have shared with me that they spent many years running from their past, but sooner or later due to gained insight or life experiences, they accepted their calling and their lives change immensely. I have been fortunate in that I knew from an earlier age that I would be a counselor. I spent many days on my front stoop listening to friends' share their problems, and many of the answers or suggestions would be impressed upon my heart to share those answers and suggestions with them.

I have been criticized by colleagues when I speak about the power of God in the work that I do because they feel that it undermines the academics of our field. But I strongly disagree, just because I believe that my interactions are driven by the very power of God, and in no way belittle the years I have spent attaining the highest degrees in my field for God is the quintessence of my degrees.

I was also able to witness this same transformation in my husband as he struggled with his "call" to the ministry. Many, many years before he thought about preaching, friends and family stated often that he would preach one day. There were some that even shared dreams that they had of him in a pulpit. We both would smile and say "never in a million years". But as the Spirit began to seriously deal with him and he prayed and mediated he announced on Mother's Day 1995 that he was accepting his "calling" to the ministry. After he came to terms with that, our family life changed.

Now mind you I thought we had a pretty good family life. He was always family oriented but when he lined up with his life mission, we all were able to line up behind him and the strength of our relationships soared. I realized that as long as he was dancing around his "calling", our family was doing the same. But once he stopped "dodging", our whole household settled down. There will always be individuals who will not support or believe in your life purpose. But that shouldn't matter because your life purpose is just that YOURS.

You need to understand that everybody does not have a right to speak into your life. All the naysayers that you will encounter are nothing compared to the naysayers that Christ endued, if you want to be like Christ, you have to do like Christ. Your purpose is that gift which you give without effort and without thought of receiving something in return. You know, the one (gift) that makes you giggle when you give it!!!

IV

PERSECUTION: A KNOWN EXPECTATION
(Math: 5:11)

Jesus boldly states that we will be persecuted, but that there is a blessing in standing firm (Math 5:11). Once we realize that the challenges we face in life serve to strengthen us in our beliefs, in our values and in our moral integrity and that we will be sustained through this transition and that a promise (benefits) waits on the other side of the bridge, most of us would willingly cross over. If we take the stance that someone or something is "doing it" to us, we are less likely to move across the bridge.

As I have grown and matured spiritually it is still surprising to me when many Christians are taken back by adversity. The Bible provides so many examples of the trials which early Christians had to endure because of their identification with Christ. Even Christ tried to provide insight to the Disciples that there is a cost to discipleship. So why are we surprised?! I have had my share of life challenges but I believed Christ when he said "I will send you a Comforter". If I wasn't going to go through or experience some uncomfortable situations why would I need a comforter? Even the word comforter denotes a sense of safety and protection. I remember spending the night at my grandmother's house, and her covering us with her comforter, there was a sense of peace that came forth; a familiarity that only came from her. The Holy Spirit does the same thing. Through diligent study of "The Word", you will learn to snuggle in the Holy Spirit's comfort.

My first experience of this "comfort" occurred at my mother's funeral. I was overwhelmed by her illness and death. My mother was a very strong personality. She always worked, managed our house and our father and never skipped a beat. When she started expressing some health concerns, none of us were particularly worried because no matter what happened in my mom's life, my mom always landed on her feet. I wasn't prepared for the manner in which her illness depleted her physically. But as I sat in our "home church" during the funeral, I knew that she had made peace with God and that she was in Heaven. This I never doubted. But I also had an acute awareness that I had shifted spiritually from when I sat in our "home church" at my father's funeral.

I have fewer clear memories of my father's funeral. During his funeral I was so lost and completely overwhelmed at the fact that he was gone. I was not the only person, my grandfather, was also overwhelmed. No parent expects to outlive their child. There was no peace or comfort in my life because I was not in relationship with Christ.

However, at my mother's funeral, I was sure of not only her future, but also of mine. I also knew that according to God's promise, I would see her again. I remember being aware of just how calm I was throughout the service, don't get me wrong, I cried and experienced a sense of loss, but the peace I experience "passeth all understanding" It is this memory that I use when facing difficult tasks. I believe that many believers fail to acknowledge God's work in their lives, so they miss it when He moves and they themselves readily take credit for that which only God can do.

One of my greatest life lessons was learning that only God can do what God can do. My favorite illustration of this is "dawn". Only God can do dawn. I travel a lot and often drive to various parts of the country, so being on the road at dawn is not an unusual experience. As I am often alone, I have time to notice those things I miss when I am traveling with some else. Dawn is one of those things you would miss. So several years ago, I started trying to "catch" dawn. You can't do that, it just appears, because only God can do "dawn". Have you ever notice that no one says I'm going to watch dawn disappear, but rather the sunrise. You would think that it is only when the sun rises can dawn appear, but that's not the case. Dawn occurs regardless of the weather, even during foggy mornings, it appears. You can sit and slowly watch the movement of the sun to anticipate the sunrise or sunset, no hints regarding dawn. So when difficult obstacles occur, dawn reminds me daily that God is and He will do whatever He wills, never all that He can.

This became a reality when I was diagnosed with ovarian cancer in spring of 2009. My worst nightmare had occurred; my mom had died of this terrible disease in 1997. She lived with me during her course of treatment, so I was very much aware of the challenges of chemotherapy and all side effects associated with it. I could not believe that this had occurred. It was my picture of "Dawn" that helped me through the acceptance of the diagnosis as well as the course of treatment which followed. No matter how bad things became, I could always count on Dawn. When I couldn't depend on the physical strength of my body, I could depend on the emergence of dawn every day. So I vowed that if God could make dawn occur on daily basis, He surely could carry me through this physical challenge. Even though I was bed-ridden through most of the treatments, whether at home or at the hospital, I could always see dawn occur. So I drew confidence by His consistency that He would also be consistence in His promises to me. He said that he would be with me always, even unto the end of the world.

V

DON'T' FOOL YOURSELF: HE DOESN'T NEED YOU
(Acts 17:22-24; 1 Cor 3:7)

In the hierarchy of the universe, you are not the deciding force but your contribution is needed and desired. The sooner we understand that we cannot hold the world hostage when we don't want to play, the more the universe benefits from our contributions because we provide them willingly and with love. I would like to ask a question, where were you when you realized that God doesn't need you.

I learned this lesson in a very difficult process. I had to live through three major losses before I came to terms with my humanness. All of these incidents involved situations with my children and out of respect for their privacy I won't go into detail but I can share the concept. Giving birth to my children is probably one of the most fulfilling aspects of my life, they were MY children. I possess them completely. As they faced their challenges, God let me know, they were His children and I was not responsible for their lives. This may sound strange, but hang in there with me. Oftentimes because of our love for others we hold them hostage to their choices. My husband and I are the best fixers in the world; I'm so good you didn't even have to ask me, I would fix it. What I learned was this interfered with God's perfect work in them. I learned to live in His will, and stay out of His way, in my life as well as others.

Proverbs tells us to "train up a child in the way he should go and when he is old, he will not depart from it." I truly was challenged by this because in my view, they did depart. I was not satisfied with many aspects of any of their lives. I often wished I could make them little again and protect them from the world. I watched over and over as they took on situations which were clearly not in their best interest. These choices were often discussed with me, we always have open communications, but THEY WOULDN'T LISTEN. But I kept trying to fix it until God put them in situations that either because of distance or other circumstances I couldn't move quickly enough to make it work for their good. But you know what; they were never out of His reach. I can testify today that his outcome was much better than any I could have imagined. He really didn't need me!

VI

WHY ARE YOU STILL OPPRESSED?

(Luke 4:16-20)

My husband was born in a little town of Boyce Louisiana, seriously a country boy. We live in the country and have had an assortment of animals but the ones I loved the most and the ones that taught me the most about "church folks" were his ducks. I have noticed over the years that the most oppressed group of people that I have had contact with are church folks, not necessary Christians, but individuals who spend a lot of time involved in church related activities. Anyway, he purchased several ducks at the same time he purchased chicks. As they were both very small, he kept them in a pen, not too far from the house. One Saturday morning after returning home from an extended trip, I was awakened by the quacking of these little friends. I turned to my husband and said "Why aren't these little creatures in the pond?"

He agreed and we got up and went outside to transplant them from the little pen to the pond, not too far from the house. We herded them down the path to the pond; they willingly went. However, it was not without a lot of quacking. We placed them in the water and they paddled around a little, I watched from the gazebo as my husband went back to the pen to bring some of their food to the pond.

My expectation was that they would be very excited about their new home- but I was wrong. They swam around for a few minutes then one by one they got out of the pond and proceeded back up the path toward the house. I followed watching over them, and after several steps, they would turn around, quack and flap their wings at me and continue their journey to the house. I couldn't believe my eyes, these ducks were walking and fussing back to limited captivity, while leaving, freedom behind and fussing at me the whole time. They proceeded to the pen, went in and were surrounded by the chicks, which at this time were also crackling in my general direction. My husband walked up puzzled, and as I walked away, I said to him "Church folks".

Christians' have been given the means to live a life of freedom but just like the ducks they prefer to be held captive. Individuals, who do profess Christ, rarely surprise me, because I have no expectation of their having an understanding of the mysteries of Christ. But leaders in the church who walk up to me and complain about a situation or question my success absolutely amazes me, because of their failure to understand that we are servicing a God of plenty, a God with awesome power, and He is no respecter of person. If you just faithfully serve Him He will give you a "pond" of freedom.

We remain in captivity as we chose not to incorporate God's principles into our daily lives and into our relationships with others. We think that as long as we go to church, sing and pray that is all that is required. If that is all you do-you will never come into the power that resides within all of us. You must tap into your source that is God, Christ said in his word that we would do more than he; we have the power to undertake any challenge and should be assured through his word that we will be successful.

VII
SO YOU THINK YOU ARE STRONGER THAN GOD
(1 Cor 10:21)

This is actual the second chapter that I wrote. I was moved to write this chapter after my blueberry pancake girlfriend lunch (you know who you are). We spent most of the time as usual sharing words of encouragement and seeking to gain a better understanding of ourselves. This is an interesting trio because on the surface you would never in a million years think that we share anything in common. We have known each other and of each other for many years but in "due season" God ordered our steps to unite together and it is doubtful to me that this bond will ever be broken. It is based on God's essence and entwine with His Holy Spirit. I'm compelled to be present for our weekly gatherings and can become quite hostile if for some life reason, that at least two of us (blueberry pancake girlfriends) can't be together. I know that this has had a positive effect on my life because both my staff and family honors this bond and encourages it because of the positive change it has made in my life and theirs. I know this is true for the other blueberry pancake girlfriends as well, because whenever we have had to cancel our get-together (only a few times) our next gathering is always one of joy and rejoicing that God allowed us to be together once again.

It is an environment in which true honesty just flows. It is one of the few places in my life I feel truly free to be just who I am. As a result of our gatherings, I am often moved to look at myself just a little closer.

This chapter began to unfold. If you haven't figured it out yet, I am a born storyteller, so slow down, don't worry, I'll get to the point.

Anyway, we were sharing over blueberry pancake brunch at the home one of my sister's house. It was an extremely cold day, not unseasonably so, but it felt cold because it had been so unseasonably warm. As we sat at the table we looked out on a lake that had that cold air look blowing on it, if you seen it you would understand what an artist delight picture view we had, what a treat it was just to see it.

It makes you appreciate the warmth, but on this particular day it wasn't just the warmth of the room, but the warmth of the fellowship. We were discussing the future of an organization that we are all involved with and we were in the process of sharing ideas and thoughts when I was asked to lead a particular task. Now mind you, my evolution in South Georgia has not been without its trials and tribulations. As I have stated elsewhere racial issues continue but there are many other issues that I hit head on (sexism, Yankeeism, role-conflict (I don't know my place), so I have walked the last several years almost invisible in my community. The pressure of living as a "strong presence" in a small town is difficult.

Additionally, when you factor in all of the other parts of me, I cannot help but thank God for His grace and mercy, and spiritual growth. So I warned our incoming president that my presence in this community on issues and programs often has served as a lightening rod-drawing undue attention and conflict. I have been told directly that my involvement has stopped projects that were supported until my involvement was noted.

This attitude had made me pretty paranoid. So I reverted back to my safety of isolation putting my energies into my work, my family and my church. Which isn't a bad thing, but it wasn't a God thing. Yes God wanted me to serve all these things, but it became very clear that there where many other things that I still had left to do. This became so very clear to me when my other sister looked at me and says too clearly-"maybe it's another season", this statement hit me like a ton of bricks. Now for some of you that may not be a profound statement, actually as I type it, it isn't, but the authority in which she stated it, it was clear.

Over the years I have learned to train my ears to become more attuned to the voice of God. In the Word, John 10:27 says "My sheep hear my voice; I know them and they do follow me". In the Book Revelation it is said, "let those who have ears hear what the spirit has to say. I am a very literal person. As I began to grow in the Word (through Bible study) I was taught to look at the context of the scripture, denoting historical relevance and current application.

For me, the question always arises, "So what would that look like for Gloria?" I understood as a young child that I had to have a personal relationship with God, but no one made that operational for me, what would a personal relationship with God be for me-how do you hang out with a Spirit?

I had to learn to communicate in a different manner. I had to learn the language of the Lord. That didn't come easy-I am a very intelligent person. I have been told this all my life, and while I didn't believe it myself, I had enough trust in those who said it to at least try to excel. So I accomplished a myriad of worldly accomplishments that demonstrated that intelligence. However, that did not transfer to Godly knowledge, yet I thought that it did. Therefore, I often planned out my actions very methodically, organized things to a compulsion and watch frantically as God taught me over and over that I had no knowledge when it came to His Word. So I tripped over my worldly knowledge daily, but as I learned to hear His voice, regardless of the messenger, those daily crashes became less frequent and less dangerous.

I don't know what your background, but I was raised in St Phillips Episcopal Church in Columbus Ohio. The current location of the church was not the original site. When I was about ten (10) years old, the church built a new structure because they were expanding the I-70 and needed the land. This was my first clash with the church hierarchy, because I didn't understand how you could demolish a building of God.

As it was an older building, it actually very regal, stately, beautiful stone building with deeply stained glass windows. I believed sincerely that God dwelled in that place and you just couldn't move God.

While I was not a part of any of the discussions, I was seriously hurt when the church building was torn down. While the new facility was beautiful and much larger, I doubted for years that God had moved; I was sure that he was as deeply disappointed as I was. At the old church our services were very regal; you knew God was in the building because of the change that occurred when people walked into the facility. There was a reverence in the building that I didn't feel moved with us. Our study of the Bible was very serious and the rituals left you with little doubt that God was looking at your every move. However, I thrived in this place; and it felt safe because God was there.

As I transitioned to young adulthood, a change in Priests changed the environment of the church. He was energetic and he made the youth a priority. He actually attended the EYC meetings and listened to our concerns. He integrated many of our ideas into the services and it was then I knew God had moved. I continued this in fellowship until my father died. I moved into a personal relationship with God, but it was weird. I learned to study about Him trying to understand how the God of my youth-the God of safety and love. could allow such an awful thing to happen. I decided at this point that I did not feel I could have a relationship with someone who did not understand what a great man my father was and how awful the world would be without his presence. I carried this in my heart for many years and through it all, God continued to love me, however, my walk depicted an attitude that I was stronger than he was. He allowed me to walk this way for many years, but when my first marriage began to fall apart; I fell on my knees and prayed like I had never prayed before.

I was like Jacob, wrestling with the protagonist. God and I wrestled over the many losses I had at age 25, we wrestled, and just like Jacob, I lost that battle, but in losing that battle I gained my eternal life. Shortly after that I reconnected with a church in Phoenix and have never wrestled with Him again.

VIII
KNOW YOUR MASTER
(3:18-28)

I have been a manager most of my adult life. It is interesting to me how little some of the individuals who have worked for me pay attention to my attributes. In fact, during interview sessions lately, I have held pre-interview appointments, to share my philosophy and strategies for our programs and work environment in attempt to "weed" out those individuals who cannot support our work "culture

There are individuals who have worked for me since I started my own practice in 1998 as well as those have worked for me only just a few days. The difference for our success is one group knows my beliefs and expectations and they deliver on that basis; whereas the other group spends their time trying to change the culture. Needless to say, but after a period of time, they leave.

The individuals, who are successful in my organization, are self-motivated, knowledgeable about our field they follow organizational policies; they have strong work ethics and are passionate toward the individuals we work with. Most of these individuals would describe our organization as "family".

Most individuals, who are not successful, will come to a job, and almost on a daily basis create havoc on the job site. This also happens in the Christian family, there are those followers who spend time in Bible study learning about the attributes of God. And as they apply what they have learned of God, to their lives, they begin to "grow" to God. Their relationship with God then becomes personal, and they understand that their behavior is a reflection or a testimony for God and an influence on others. But those those just show up and fail to gain an understanding about Gods' attributes, are unable to manifest righteous behaviors in their lives mainly because they don't know who God is.

When you have individuals who have to investigate the needs of others through committees they don't understand the story of the Good Samaritan. God does not just take care of our emergency, he provides for our needs before we even know the need exist. The Good Samaritan demonstrated with his actions our purpose in life, to care for your fellow man. The Word says that at every opportunity-do good. It doesn't say wait until someone asks.

I have been a member of many different churches throughout my life and it has always been interesting to me how they handle requests from members and other individuals who are in need. There seems to be a preoccupation with being "taken advantage of" by deadbeats. They justify the need to "investigate" because some individuals are just lazy and won't do anything to help them. On an occasion, this spirit manifested itself in a church we were involved and there had been a request from an individual for food. The deacon through whom the request was made to the church for assistance stated the man had called him by phone twenty-one (21) times and the church needed to make a decision so this man "would quit bothering me". I watched and listen as the discussion centered around who knew the man, did anyone know whether or not he was on drugs, etc. I watched and listened for about 15 minutes and then asked "what difference does it make?" The church had a benevolent obligation to assist. I was challenged by everyone in the room, and because I had worked for at the time in law enforcement, I knew better than most, how many deadbeats and con men were out there. I acknowledged their points but promised them that no deadbeat or con men would ask twenty-one

(21) times for assistance, they would have moved on by this time, rather that this was clearly an individual who was hungry. I also suggested that God doesn't always move through the obvious. I used their fear to make a point. I told them suppose the man was a "con man or deadbeat", that if the church help this individual, he would probably go out and talk about the church and you don't know who that would move to come to the church for true relief. I also pointed out that in the story of the Good Samaritan, the man's current and future needs were met and not once was there a question about how he got in his situation. I reminded them that we are blessed so that we can be a blessing to others. While you are having committee meetings and investigations, God's Children are hungry and cold. I also asked if God held a committee meeting for you prior to his going to the Cross, what would have been the outcome?

DO AS I HAVE DONE
(John 13:1-16)

In this Scripture reading, John provides an account of Jesus washing the feet of the disciples. During this writing, this task would be considered one of the lowly responsibilities to perform in a household, yet Jesus washed their feet to demonstrate the attitude needed to be a follower of Him. He teaches them knowing that they have not yet matured spiritually to have a true understanding of what it is that He is doing.

Most of the time this Scripture has been taught in my presence, it is from the point that to be a servant you must serve. However, I believe an important aspect of this teaching was that His serving them provided a connection to Him that could not occur without His serving them. Jesus clearly says "Unless I wash you, you have no part with me". The commentaries that I have read regarding this point all stress the "spiritual cleansing". This is a point I challenge, perhaps Jesus was establishing the foundation of a relationship between the servant and his service. Simply saying -that to be a part of me, service is required.

During my illness with ovarian cancer, my husband cared for my every need. He only left my side to preach on Sundays and conduct Wednesday night Bible studies. He accompanied me to every doctor's appointment; sat at my side at the hospital, and prepared meals for me on a daily basis. My children assisted him but he was clear to everyone, "this is my wife, I will care for her". When someone cares for you their behaviors depict that. I have always known that he would support me, he always has, but the level of care, patience, and concern that he displayed everyday was amazing to me. He served me and through his service to me our relationship grew bountifully. I was sharing this with my younger daughter stating how good it felt, how secure I felt in his care and she stated "it's the first time you have allowed him to care for you". Ouch, I had to step back and reflect on this statement, realizing how true it is.

We fail to allow God to care for us. We are too busy trying to establish our own righteousness. We are trapped by the demands of our society to succeed. This success is measured by the amount of stuff we have, our educational credentials, and our positions on our jobs. But Solomon told us that this is all vanity, it will all pass away.

Jesus is trying to get us to understand that the only calling we have is to serve one another. Whatever your gift, use it to serve your fellow man.

X

WHAT "KINDA" DIRT ARE YOU?
(Matt 13:3-23)

This Scripture references the parables of the seed. Most of us have heard this story many times to understand that it is one that we often dismiss when it is presented in church settings. We know that Jesus used parables to teach the disciples and people of that time to help them gain understanding of biblical principles. We know that the definition of a parable is an earthly example of divine truth. So in this teaching Jesus is speaking to farmers and uses a subject that He knows they will understand-dirt and seed. He tells of four different types of dirt, but does not describe the type of seed. When I look at the application of this lesson, I understand that the dirt is examples of our hearts and the seed is the word of God. However, I believe that there is an even more direct and deeper application of this parable.

Now I would never say that my husband and I are farmers however, he does have a garden that he tends on regular basis and we feed a great number of people out of that garden. I watch him till (prepare) the land every season to get ready to plant. Regardless of the condition of the land, prior to sowing the seed, the sower must be ready. The seed is not prepped, the land is. The Word of God is not prepped, your heart is. In order to get ready to receive the word (seed) you must identify – what type of dirt are you? I said in an earlier chapter that the most dangerous people are people who don't know what they don't know. This applies to this parable. If you don't acknowledge the condition of your heart, you can prepare it for the word. Jesus gives us a clear example or checklist we can use to determine the condition of our heart.

First, He speaks about the wayside-this is seed that isn't even purposely laid or received. There are many who are in our congregations and families who attend services but have no purpose for the word. If it "hits" them fine, but their reaction to the Word is often defensive. You will hear comments like-"I hate coming because he is always talking about me" or "They talk about the same thing every time I come". This depicts an attitude (prep) of arrogance that the word of God is aimlessly applied to our life. To prepare this type of soil often results in a tragic incident in their life for them to become engaged in the process. This individual finds it difficult to accept the word of God as true and living, their perspective of the Word is "back then, or those people". They may respond to emotional pleas but are soon distracted as indicated by the parable where they are devoured by the birds. Old folks used to say if you don't stand for something you will fall for anything, this describes these individuals.

"Some fell on the stony places", it is difficult to penetrate stone. I have been fortunate to travel to many places, most recently to Egypt and the Great Pyramids, Acropolis, Mars Hill, and all the buildings are made out of stone. As we walked these steps of stone and marble, even after thousands of years, these steps, while worn, were still adequate for us to travel and view these areas. As I sat and watch literally thousands of people walk this area with us I was amazed that these steps could handle the amount of traffic they obvious had. That's how hard some individual's hearts are to the Word God. We all have had individuals, family and friends, who we have witnessed the word and testimony of God and amazed that they could not get it, or if they did, could not maintain it. We see members start out with good intentions but so they become absent from our services or activities because they didn't get "rooted" in the word. 2 Timothy 2:15 tells us to study to show ourselves approved unto God a workman that needed not to be ashamed, rightly dividing the

Word of Truth. It's not enough to listen to the word, study it provides the preparation.

The third type of dirt is good dirt, but it has been invested t ...orns and was devoured by the thorns. Your associations are important, this is very important because we are encouraged to testify and witness to others about God, however, if you surround yourself with individuals who have no knowledge of God, you will be choked out. So the problem is not your heart, but your associates.

But the good ground, that ground which is rich, you can tell good ground by the color, texture, even the smell. People should be able to see your "dirt" and know it's good. This the only ground that reaps a lasting harvests. But even so, the harvest is not the same. He gives examples of different levels of increase; the emphasis is that this is the only dirt which reaps a healthy harvest. A lasting harvest. So the question, what "kinda" dirt are you? Is answered by the harvest you have produced. As you look around your life, ask yourself, what type of fruit have I produced?

XI
SLAVERY THAT FREES
(Ex 21:1; Col 1:13)

The Leviticus law clearly defined the relationship between the slaves and their masters during this time. The Bible spells out the relationship between the master and the slave and subsequent family members. It speaks of the relationship between the master and the children of the slaves. Basically, they belong to their master with no hope of release even after the seventh year, because they came to the master through the relationship with the family as a slave. The slave could stay with his family only to remain in servitude. The decisions regarding the welfare of the slave and his family were rested with the master.

We have current day examples of slavery that has occurred around this world. We have world leaders, past and present, who have subjected individuals to horrific crimes against humanity. We have history books full of examples of how one group of people treated another group of people with injustice, torture, and even death. As I write this book, Greece, Egypt, Tunisia, Libya are all having civic unrest because of the manner in which the leaders have treated the people. Slavery has been a part of our world for long time.

But in Christ we have been released from slavery of sin through our relationship with him. In the relationship between the slave and his master, there is an acknowledgement that will is not an issue. This is something we miss in our relationship with God. We have heard the story where Christ says "not my will Lord, but yours". But we don't apply this to our lives. We have a vision in our head that God needs to be told how to work out the problems, or how a situation should be resolved, however, that is completely contrary to the attributes of God identified in the Bible. The God that we serve is eternal, omnipotent, omniscient, and omnipresent. He is everywhere and knows everything and has all power. If we truly trust Him, that worry no longer controls our lives because we recognize-He's got your back! I experienced this truly when I became ill and was unable to work. I had my own business and staff but the illness was sudden and unexpected. (Like most of his tests). I released all concerns to Him because I was too physically weak to take them on. I have prayed every day since then to stay in His will and out of His way.

In biblical times, slavery was used in many ways, indebtedness, loss of battles, etc. The examples we have read all speak to the cruelty of man toward his fellow man. Actually God allowed the Israelites to suffer in slavery as a result of their disobedience. But these are all acts under the hand of man; the type of slavery that I speak is under the hand of God. In God's hand, there is not corruption, cruelty, or division. In God's hand there is love, strength, peace, joy, longsuffering, and patience. Under God's hand, the challenges of the world are encompassed by the comfort of the Holy Spirit. When you become a slave for Christ, you know that the Great Master will ensure that all your needs and desires are provided as long as you remain in his will. The enemy gets us distracted on the words slavery, servitude, submission, deceiving us to believe that these words represent weakness. When in reality, it is through this weakness that God and Christ manifest their power and love for us. That is why most people do not "get it" until they are in a situation where their only option is God. But once the crisis is over, it's business as usual. That's the deception, business is never usual when you serve God. When you walk in His will everyday you experience the miracle of Him, you experience the "nowness" of His presence. Nowness is my word for the immediacy of God. When God speaks things happen. Yes sometimes there may be a delay, but more often than not the miracle happens right in front of us but we are so distracted by daily busyness, we miss it. Today I walk in the "nowness" of Christ, I truly expect a miracle everyday and I am never disappointed

XII
WHAT IS YOUR PURPOSE?
(Romans 8:28)

This is one of the first Scriptures that caught my eye, heart and soul. I don't know what age I was, but if any Scripture in the Word held the most meaning in my life it would be this "For I know that everything works to the good of those who love God and are called according to his purpose". I have always known that I had a special purpose to fulfill. However, I didn't quite understand what that purpose was. I have always "walked to a different drum." I have never viewed the world through worldly glasses. Even when I was not truly following God's word, I always knew that I was unique in my observations of issues and challenges. I truly believe that I could accomplish anything if I tried, the Word clearly states "I can do all things through Christ that strengthened me" Philippians 4:13. So when I received comments like "how can you do that" or "how did you do that" it was puzzling because God's word clearly states what happens when He directs your path (Pro 3:5). The problem isn't finding your path, the problem is listening to God and obeying his word, the path becomes very clear when you practice these principles. This particular scripture gives reassurance to know that no matter what is happening around you, no matter what people are saying, if you are dedicated to God, it will work out for your good. This doesn't mean that you will get everything you want; rather you will receive things necessary for your good. Good is described in this scripture as "those who love God and are called according to his purpose".

The first time I searched the scriptures for a current application I was 15 years old and my first boyfriend had been killed in a car accident. His mother was a very kind woman who taught me a great deal about life in a very short period of time. Despite her great loss she was very sensitive to the loss that I was experiencing. Unlike most of the adults around me, she understood just how much I cared for her son and did not minimize those feelings because of my age. Instead she honored me by allowing me to select the Scriptures that would be inscribed on his headstone. Prior to this I had not looked into the Scriptures without being directed either in Bible study or Sunday School. Even my personal study was directed by books that my father and grandmother had given me. I had never truly searched the scriptures through the Holy Spirit. So I prayed and asked the Lord to guide me and he lead me to Matthew 20:16 which reads "So the last will be first and the first last, for many are called but few are chosen". We used the last part of this scripture because I felt he was selected by God for a specific work and he had accomplished his work and was now in the presence of God. Even at the young age of 16, he impacted many, many lives through his love and kindness and willingness to serve.

So my first duty is to love God. He says in his word "if you love me, you will keep my commandments" (John 14:15). He also told Peter that if Peter loved Christ he would feed his flock. He wasn't referring to actual food but rather feeding them the Word. This journey is quite simple once you realize that your entire purpose is to "serve you one another". Christians have become "of the world" in their quest to have and be "more". God gives us a clear message about stuff, he says "seek ye first the kingdom of righteousness and all these things will be added unto you." Once you follow his Word, the importance of things changes in your life, your focus is Christ-centered. After you dedicate all your efforts to service, God begins to bless you with material things because you no longer worship or strive for them rather your efforts are focused on service of others. Matthew 25:21 says "Well, done good and faithful servant, you have been faithful over a few things, I will make you ruler over many things, Enter into the joy of your Lord". Often the interpretation applied to this Scripture is that when you die God will bless you. I suggest very strongly and use my life as a testimony, if you are faithful to Him here in your service to others you can enjoy his joy (authority) now.

I live in a home that I could not have imagined as a child or young adult, but God put a team of professionals together who fulfill his vision for me. Every time I drive up to my home even after living there for over 15 years. I am amazed at what God has given me. The cars that I dreamed of driving are nothing compared to what God has provided. Once I stopped "lusting" for these things, he gave them to me willingly.

During my recuperation from my cancer, I learned to truly appreciate the simplicity of God's Word and was drawn to simplify things in my life. I downsized my business but also downsized my need for things.

When asked the rich man asked what he needed to do to enjoy a relationship with Christ, he was told to leave all his possessions and follow Him. The rich man dropped his head and walked away. Too many of us have dropped our heads and walked away just like the rich man. We may be in the room (sitting in the church) but we are not in the game (serving ye one another). What have you done lately?

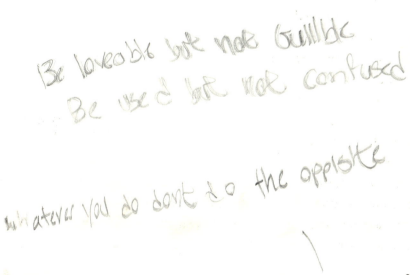

Be loveable but not Gullible
Be used but not confused

whatever you do dont do the oppisite

XIII

ARE YOU WORTHY OF THE GOSPEL

(Philippians 1:27-30)

There appears to be a misunderstanding of the purpose of the Gospel message. Many individuals today view religion as a means to improve their lives as well as receive many benefits. This is in fact true however; the higher calling is to demonstrate the true Word of God in our behaviors and actions.

I have been a manager most of my life, an entrepreneur to be exact. I have started three business and employed individuals to conduct these various business affairs. All the individuals that came to work for me did not come for the same reason. Some came because they needed a job (paycheck); some came because they heard about the work I was doing; some came just "to see" what I was doing; some came to "steal" what I was doing; some came because they had a genuine interest in the type of work I was doing; and some came because of the relationships that we had developed and they were there to support me. The overall mission of the organization was similar, but the tasks and opportunities varied based on their motivations and intentions. Many times I would be called upon to make presentations at various locations and times, and if I had a conflict in my schedule or would be overbooked, I knew that everyone that worked for me could not necessarily represent me at those meetings. Their motives were not true and for oftentimes they would misrepresent our mission by making their own spins. While others did not have enough understanding of the overall mission to be able to properly represent the organization.

This is true for Christians. Many call themselves Christians, but they are not worthy to carry the message because their motivations and/or intentions are not true to the Word of God. God clearly states in these verses that we must have the same mind in ourselves that He had. Clearly, Jesus demonstrates His only desire to fulfill the will of His Father. Some individuals use their Christianity to gain their own desires (Romans 10). These individuals have lost the servant attitude; they would rather be served that to serve. In fact many have no intentions of serving others. Being a minister's wife has placed me in many different types of settings with other ministers and their wives. The attitude of service is not always present. I have heard comments where the ministers and their wives expect special services rather than provide services. Even in our own experience we have been challenged by members who "want to do everything" for their pastor. We love the gesture of love but have really had to educate our members of God's attitude toward service. You also have individuals who "position" themselves in Christian settings to solely benefit from the service of others.

XIV

DON'T LET GOD PUT YOUR BUSINESS IN THE STREET
(2 Chro 7:21-22)

"And as for this house, which is exalted, everyone who passes by it will be astonished and say, why has the Lord done thus to this land and this house. Then they will answer "Because they forsook the Lord God of their fathers who brought them out of the land of Egypt and embraced other gods, and worshipped them and served, therefore He has brought this entire calamity on them..."

As I stated initially, this book has evolved over several years. This chapter is being written in April 2010 following my dance with ovarian cancer. God gave me the titles to these chapters over 10 years ago. This title was one that I embraced but was confident that God was going to have me write this chapter about people who had entered my life, because when I started writing this book, I was ok with Him. Well let me tell you God has no use for "ok".

I awoke about 1:00 am with a clear vision of the words that are to go into this chapter. There is no editing of these words by me or anyone else. God put my business-literally in the street. When I woke up to write this chapter, I had to first find which laptop or zip drive I had the latest version, never found it-just started writing. The outline that I developed included all the titles that God had given me and the scripture that spurned the title. When I re-read the scriptures referenced above and I couldn't help but laugh. This chapter really is all about me.

I confess here and now that I was so wrapped up in my own talents and abilities, that while I confessed God daily, witnessed to others about the miraculous things he had done and was doing in my life-I was a fraud. I believed everything that I said to others, but I didn't know that I believed it until I heard the words cancer, specifically ovarian cancer. It crippled everything that I knew. It had brought a special fear in my heart because I had watched it destroy my mother-it was my greatest fear and based on all that was told me by the professionals and individuals-it was hopeless. But when I realized what was actually happening, it was impossible to embrace these negatives thoughts and ideas because my God is a God of hope, so how could I be hopeless, but let's start at the beginning of this experience.

There were several things that I struggled with, envy, pride, resentments and anger. At the time I began writing this book, most people, particular my Christian family had not seen this side of me primarily because I became very astute on how to mask these behaviors. But one Sunday, envy crept boldly into my heart, as I was teaching a Sunday School class on Job and was taken back by the fact that God had "smiled" about Job. That stuck in my spirit more that I would like to admit, I began to manifest the desire that I wanted God to smile on me just like he smiled on Job-in my ignorance I had no idea what I was releasing in to my life. I have always had a belief about the spoken word (but I did not know just how much I believed it until this challenged unfolded).

The other behavior that I held onto was pride which manifested itself in my life in the form of vanity. I became good about masking it by saying that the things that I had accumulated were because of how well I served God-even quoting scripture that if you put him first, he will give you the desires of your heart-I even had ministers using the same application. Again, I didn't realize what I was releasing into my life.

The other behavior that I had obtained a PhD in was gathering resentments-in fact I became so good at this, I had my own resentment posse- I had so many resentments that I needed other people to help me in gathering them and provided validation on the many things I had been wronged. I carried these in my heart until they manifested themselves physically in my body. Even during my health challenge, I was betrayed by several individuals who I entrusted. But I had begun to honestly view this issue and was able to heal of the betrayal without developing the resentment that I would normally have masked. It was funny because my posse was on their job-they developed the strategy for the resentment for me and when I told them that I had already forgiven the individual or situation and had asked God's mercy on them, they were dumfounded. What's even better, my posse took their horses and left, I pray that if they read this they will unsaddle those resentment ponies and put them out to pasture, they need a rest.

Finally, I struggled with anger; nobody gets angrier quicker than I do. You've seen commercial ads that talk about going from 0-60 in so many seconds-I didn't need a second. Now I'm not a loud angry person. I had learned to change that-it didn't get me the results that I wanted, besides everyone ignored loud angry black women-there were so many of us. I adopted the silent approach-non verbals were my forte. I learned to maneuver through systems with underlying anger fueling me. I learned that getting angry wasn't the problem; it was the action that I took when I became angry. This was the only time that I manifested patience, waiting to get even.

During my illness because my physical body became so weak, I began astutely aware of how much energy it takes to fuel that type of angry. I wish that I could say that I had a divine intervention and God spoke wise words to me, but in reality I was too weak to maintain pride, anger, resentments or envy. It took everything out of me just to sit up in the bed. Now I didn't learn this quickly, I had several setbacks which were attributed to stress that surrounded these emotions. I had to learn to deal with the source of the emotion in a spiritual manner because I could no longer mask these emotions.

These behaviors I had refocused to be more socially acceptable but they would never be acceptable to God. It was clear to me during my physical challenge that I was not living the standard God required because I still manifested these behaviors and clearly they are not of God. So I became a student again openly asking God to teach me and guide me, I literally submerged myself in scriptures all day-I read, had my husband read to me or listen to cd with only the scriptures related to healing.

During this time, I was unable to do much of anything-this is when my business was "in the street". People looked at me just like Job and asked similar (just updated questions) "why is this happening to her-I thought she was a strong Christian" "you know this is happening to her because she is a Christian-Satan's attacking her" on and on it went. But God did not validate these in my spirit. What resonated in my heart was not what I was going through but how I was going through it. Did I manifest the things that I had professed those many years and even I was surprised by the answer-yes I did. During this period I felt pain that I never knew, and despite all of the medications that was provided, the only thing that provided complete relief was listening to a CD that was given to me by a friend which consist of readings of the "healing scriptures. Each one of the scriptures included spoke about the healing power of God.

As I listened to this daily during this period, immediately when I arose and before I went to bed, I listened to this CD; when the pain was so great, I listened to this CD, I recorded it in my car and every time I get in my car, I listened to this CD, As time went on, the pain was less present in my mind, what captured my attention was the power contained within his word. It challegened me- Did I truly believe- if I did-this was nothing to be worried about or to fear, because God had already, through his Word, addressed any need I had. I understood that this diagnosis was not the sum of me, rather a bump in the road, the road I was to travel to become more and more close to Him. The road that was taking to places I had not even imagined, and for that I am thankful.

XV
A STANDARD TO LIVE BY
(Philippians 4:8-20)

As I have grown in Christ, in his mercy and grace, I become curious about the behaviors that we choose to display when it is clear what standards Christ has developed for us. As I began to listen to those true things it was easier to identify the false things-I was less likely to get distracted by gossip, envies', resentments that occur from focusing on those false things. As I focused on the honest things-what were my motivations for the things I was doing-not what others were doing, but me. I recognized how many activities I was involved in were not for the glory of God; they weren't for the glory of me; but rather, they were tied to individuals and organizations whose underlying positions were counter to those of God. I realized that many in their own ignorance were being driven by reasons that were less honest and I was unevenly yoked with them. I honestly shared this information prior to my ending the relationships so that they were done decent and in order and it helped me to maintain my integrity with God.

Much of my anger was the result of the injustices that I had experienced in the many roles that had been placed upon me, many of which I carried too long. These roles came with expectations and standards which were bread in dishonesty. Oftentimes my rationale for staying involved was the belief that I could change people from becoming as corrupt as they were. While I did not participate in many activities my awareness of these activities and my unwillingness to challenge these decisions resulted in corruption of my mind, it again, separated me from the peace promised by God. This realization again resulted in severing off many relationships that were not grounded in the Word of God. Once you honestly deal with you own dishonest beliefs, it's not too difficult to gain understanding and insight into the behaviors of others.

Most things are pure, because of their simple make-up. The oneness of the "thing" makes it pure; once you add something to the "thing" it is no longer pure. This application was actually the most difficult because it required a change in mindset that did not occur until I was extremely ill. During this period, I discovered that any deviation from my simple routine resulted in serious medical issues. My standards became biblically based, rather than society-based.

XVI
ONE NOTE
(1 Cor 12:12-27)

As I have stated previously, my profession is counseling. I have worked in this field many years. I have often paralleled for myself the Christian journey with those of many of the clients I have treated over the years. In working with individuals who have mental health issues, raising their awareness to the existence of a problem is half the battle. It is difficult if not impossible to treat someone who doesn't believe they have a problem, even more difficult when they don't know that they don't know. Christians often have this problem because they assume their understanding of the Word is deeper that what it actually is. I am a very concrete thinker and it has challenged me in many areas but nowhere more so that studying the Bible. This chapter speaks of many parts, however, there is only one whole. This passage of Scripture is rarely visible in the body of Christ. There is more division in our communities on Sunday morning that any other day of the week. We speak of one body, whatever the different denominations have created divisions that most people don't even understand. I have always been an advocate of history, so why something is practiced a certain way is important because if I understand the beginning, it gives me more insight into the application. In this passage of Scriptures Paul is trying to give insight into the purpose of the different gifts, to edify the body of Christ and to glorify God. What I have observed in various settings is these gifts are used to glorify men and divide the body of Christ. If I applied these practices to my clinical setting, I would diagnosis the church as Schizophrenic-functioning in a delusional paranoid state as if their realty has not been altered by their disease. When you look at the lives that Christ and his disciples displayed, it reflected what they spoke about in their teachings. Can we say the same for us? Do we walk in the same manner that we talk? How can we speak about service when all we expect is to be served? How can we speak about benevolence (giving) when all we expect is to receive? In Mathew 12 Christ speaks about the division of the house, cannot stand, is that not reflected in our religious culture now? If your spiritual life is divided from your secular life, you will not stand. I believe that one of my greatest gifts is I know what I know, but more importantly, I know what I don't know. But I know that there is One that knows it all.

XVII

A PRESCRIPTION FOR A DYING LOVE

(2 Chron 7:14)

Another 3:00 a.m. discussion, this time it only took me forty minutes to get up and begin writing. This Scripture is one that my husband quotes more often than not when he rises to preach the Gospel. It is a very powerful scripture (as they all are) but this morning the Lord led me to this particular Scripture to deal with the issue of forgiveness. When I woke up this morning, I laid in the bed, hoping I was just turning over, but after several bouts of tossing I realize that the Lord was attempting to deal with my spirit and forgiveness arose yet again. As it rose, I began to pull out my list of betrayals to see "who do I need to forgive" Understand that this list did not consists of those I had betrayed, yet those that had betrayed me (in my opinion). The model prayer flashed across my spirit, that's when I knew it was time to get up., so here we go.

If-this word was explained to me all through school as a conditional term, dependent on something in order for whatever follows to become a reality. So in reading this scripture, you must make a decision to either agree to the condition or not. It's that simple.

My-denotes ownership. It represents identification. While I have worked with many children and refer to them sometimes as mine, there are three children who belong to me (as much as another can belong to another). I created these children through the birth process; there is a connection with them that I don't share with another individual on this earth. A connection that continues even after death as I learned through the lost of my mother and father; grandparents and other elders in my life.My experiences with them rests on the instinctual knowledge that I have about them, it comes from that connection of creation. This is similar to the relationship we have with God. He knows us in a way that no other knows because he caused us to be. In addition, when we were yet sinners, he died for us. This occurred whether we accept it or not. However, in this scripture until we do accept it (principles, laws, statues, precepts), it does not refer to us, but if we do, what power we posses and do not utilize. In knowing this how can we withhold forgiveness from anyone, if we acknowledge how unworthy we are of God's forgiveness of us.

People-this may not appear to need an explanation, but it does. When we think of this word we acknowledge that people do not include plants and animals. People were made in the very image of God-free will, conscience. In other words, we make a conscious decision everyday to either display behaviors associated with people, or animals or plants. I'm not saying that we become these things; rather we chose to act as one or the other. When I hear the news of violence against innocent children, starvation horrific acts against the most vulnerable, I think of the animal species where only the strong survive. That is not the order of God's people. In the word he tells over and over that we are to care for one another-bare one another's burdens, brother's keeper, the strong must bear the infirmities of the weak, of much is given much is expected-on and on. So with this identification comes along responsibility for one another. A responsibility to care only because another exists is sufficient for the true Christian As I am writing this particular chapter I received an email inviting me to join a computer database so that you can check and see what services an individual may be receiving from other organizations. What purpose does this serve the Christians? This reminds me of David's desire to count the number in his kingdom when God specifically told him not to; but he did anyway. What is the purpose, is this contrary to Jesus' charge to love ye one another; or the strong are to bear the infirmities of the weak. There is no mention of the need to see if others are helping. When you care for something, it requires effort and attention. It requires action-God's people are people of action. True believers don't need to be prompted to fulfill his will. They are the peacemakers-not people who just let it go. They move forward to invite peace into a situation. We are a people who have a spirit of reconciliation.

Who-another clarifier, these words refer to a group out of a larger group? Specific behaviors are sure to follow,

Called-this represents a divine interaction with God and his children. This represents a personal interaction with God. Can you remember playing as a child, maybe down the street or out in a field, and you heard in a distance your name being called. There was no doubt in your mind when you heard your name that you were being called. Even if there were other children in the area who had your name, when you parent called you, you knew that they were calling only you and often knew what they were calling you for, the only questions arose was whether or not you were going to answer or respond.

By-another level of identification, you can think of this scripture as a funnel. It may surprise many who know me professionally, but I'm a pretty good cook. Every so often I invite a group over to break the stereotype that you can't have a successful career and function in the home also. Anyway a funnel is often used to pour something from a large container into a smaller container. The concept is that by using the funnel you are less likely to spill the contents. This term by is a funnel term. You see if you don't fit into this smaller container, this doesn't apply. This is where a lot of Christians are misled. Satan has us to believe that all scripture applies to us if we say we believe. As usual that is partially true. Satan is an expert at half-truths. He got an early start in the garden. But the Word says that we must not only be a hearer (believer) of the Word, but we must be a doer of the Word (James 1:22). So we must, through our changed behavior (mindset) fit into this funnel.

My-another level of possession, in both incidents this word is capitalized which lets us know that God himself is speaking here. He is again staking claim to those who will receive the benefit of this particular Scripture

Name-Too many Christians do not understand God's name. They can rattle off many of the labels associated with God, but they do not understand his name. What I mean by this is with each label or title referenced to God, there comes a benefit. You see God is not like us, He is true to his Word. So when he says that He will be your provider, He really means it. The problem comes along when we give God advice. I remember a particular time when I was being persecuted by Satan and I had just left my bank. I had arrived with a very organized plan to request additional funds for operations and outstanding IRS payroll taxes (another whole book) anyway I must have looked terribly ill and the vice president of the bank took one look at me and had me pick up a book by Max Lucado (one of my favorite writers) entitled Grace-a devotional. He told me to look at certain date in the book; I immediately corrected him by telling him what the correct date was. He simply smiled and said I know, but I want you to look at the date that I gave you. When I did after reading the first sentence, I broke down in tears and cried like I had never cried before. After he ministered to my spirit, I left his office and drove straight to the bookstore and purchased one copy for myself and several other copies because I know that whenever God teaches me a lesson He always sends some to me that needs the same lesson, I learned this early in my life from my grandmother who had a very deep benevolent spirit, she lived the Word. Anyway, after getting my book, I drove to Atlanta and as usual I was listening to a Christian satellite station but for the first 1 ½ hours on the road, I only heard songs of praise. Now mind you I never did give the banker my request, I only received his ministry to my spirit. But as I was passing a church that I pass going and coming on my trips to Atlanta- the marquee outside the church stated, "Stop giving God instructions and follow His directions". Obedience is a characteristic of God's child. The universe is obedient to the will of God. I don't believe that there is any incident in history where the Sun attempted to rise in the west and set in the east. My husband is a country boy so we have had several difference types of animals on our property. It's interesting that with the exception of man, nature follows the order of God. He says he is not a God of confusion, but I spend most of my day working with individuals through acts of disobedience to Gods will in their lives, are living lives of confusion. They often share with me "I know what I should be doing I just don't"; just like the little kid who ignores his mother's voice. A child will display some of the characteristics and traits of the parent, even if they have not been raised by the parent. My husband and I parented nine children. When we married he had three, I had three and then we raised three grandchildren. Even though we lived thousands of miles from their other parent(s); as they got older they displayed some of the traits and characteristics of the other parent. A dear friend of ours who was a principal and involved with the school system for 40 years says all the time "genes don't lie". Our moral DNA was breathed into us when Adam was formed, what is your understanding of God's name and how does that show up in your life? A dear friend said to me one time- either you believe God or you believe he is a liar. This spoke directly into my soul as I was worried about my mounting business, and family problems. But God says that through Christ I can do all things and sometimes that is nothing. He says that when you have done all you can to stand-just stand. He shares the extent of His power with use in this Scripture. When we get to the point we can't go on-that's when He steps in-His strength begins at the end of ours.

Would-denotes obedience. He didn't say should, could, but would. There needs to be a willingness to follow the directions of the Word.

Once I accepted this, life became so much simpler. It was so freeing to become a slave to God's Word. No matter what the world circumstances are, God has it handled. I don't have to understand the process, means to the end; I just know that whatever the process involves, it is for my good.

Humble-this is one of the most misunderstood words I believe in the Christian world. We have used this term simultaneously with weakness. Humbleness acknowledges that you really believe God is who He says He is, you recognize and accept that He knows more than you and that there is a better good than what you may want at a particular time. I am so thankful to God today that He did not give me all the things that I "thought" I had to have or I would die.

Themselves-again this is an identified group of people. This speaks to those individuals who identify with the almighty God. This is important because not just gangs, sorority, fraternities, political and other social organizations have specific identifications. So does God's people. These are people who honor the very idea that there is something (GOD) in the universe that is in control. These are a people of hope and possibility. These are a people of peace and patience. These are a people of faith and obedience-who do the right thing solely because it is the right to do. In the word Paul speaks about a peculiar people. We are different than the world; we stand out when looking at the behaviors of the world. We should be different. The familiar Scriptures referenced as often as "B" attitudes denotes the characteristics that Christians out to demonstrate.

Poor in spirit-denotes a humble attitude, position and prosperity become less important. Jesus says in the Sermon on the Mount that only the poor in spirit will see Him. If you have an arrogant or proudful spirit God cannot use you because you believe that your aspirations and successes are because of your abilities not because of God's grace.

If you have not or are not experiencing these types of situations in your life, you are not referenced in this passage. This is important because many individuals who are associated with the body of Christ believe that that association is all that is needed. Just yesterday, my husband and I were speaking with gentlemen outside church following services. We had visited another church and as we fellowshipped outside, we were speaking about the need to have a personal relationship with God. He used the analogy of having his mother and grandmother pray for him while he was young but at a certain time in his life he needed to start praying for himself. He used a relay race and the importance of having the baton in your hand when you cross the finish line. This was so graphic for me that he used this race as an example. We have been trained by many in our families, schools etc about the need to have God in our lives, yet we don't personally take responsibility for that, relying on others to pray for us. Eternity, regardless of your age is in front of you, that finish line is approaching whether you move forward or not. The Word says that there is an appointed time for every man to die and after death comes judgment (Hebrews 9:27). The baton (life you lived) will cross that line with you. The Bible clearly lays out those behaviors that will be taken into account.

And-this is a conjunction according to my English teachers. It is clear and specific when this word shows up it means I must also do what falls before it and what falls after it. Whatever the content of the sentence if I don't do both parts the sentence is irrelevant. This is a formula for success; you can think of this word as the plus sign in an equation.

Pray-As I have matured spiritually, I have been amazed how difficult many people find prayer. I was fortunate in that I was raised in a household where I saw everyone in my family pray. Even those who were not active in a church knew to pray prior to eating and said prayers at night. As a single mother raising three young children, we often prayed together prior to leaving the house for the day and would receive calls from my children throughout the day to pray for them or their friends as the challenges of adolescents started up showing up. I always honored their requests but encouraged them to express their concerns as I prayed with them. As my involvement in church situations grew, I noticed that many people really did not know how to pray. I was included. After a Bible study of the model prayer (often referred to as the Lord's Prayer) I realized that God had an expectation on how to be approached during prayer. I also realized that many of my prayers were inappropriate in their nature. God is not going to answer a negative prayer, a prayer of vengeance or revenge. While He creates situation where that may occur, it's according to Him- vengeance is mine says the Lord. I also realized that I need to have the right attitude when I prayed; primarily I need to believe that what I pray for God will provide.

And-this indicates while prayer is important, it is not the only necessity in this formula. God is clearly stating to us that there are requirements to get His attention and if we expect success, we must follow the formula.

Seek-this is not to be confused with words such as looking, checking out, checking in, finding the time. This is about making the priority of being in connection with God. I have been moved over the past couple weeks that God wanted me to fast over the Lent season. In the past I have fasted for guidance, clarification, a multitude of things. Most recently the Lord indicated that I needed to fast during the upcoming season Journal prayers 3 times through day; rest 3 days per day (exercise, meditation, stress reduction) The purpose of any fast is to either gain insight into God's plan or cleansing. Either way it requires a concerted effort to move closer in your relationship with God Jesus himself told the disciples that some things cannot be obtained without prayer and fasting. Both of these are a personal interaction with God.

Purposeful effort to gain insight into God's plan in your life is not a casual activity; it's not something that happens by accident. Seeking occurs when you lose your car keys and you are attempting to get to work on time. Everyone at one point in time has misplaced their car keys. As time runs down, you not only look but you solicit support from others There has been times in my household when either my husband or I lose our keys and everybody needs to look until they are found. That should be our efforts on a daily basis. We should seek God until we find Him, if we cannot locate Him by ourselves we need to ask for others support. We should look in obvious places and not so obvious places. When my husband looses his keys it is often a greater challenge because he so tall that eye level for him is different than for the rest of the house. Sometimes in the craziness of the church, especially when we think we looked everywhere, we stop take a deep breath and look again, and invariably the keys are in a obvious place, in plain sight. The Word of God is the same, we will swear up and down that we looked there but didn't see, but lo and behold, there they are. So should be our efforts in gaining insight into seeking God.

My-another sign of possession. It's almost like stalking God, we should look everywhere for Him, nothing else will do. The key to Satan is seeking God. The Bible states over and over that when God is present, Satan must flee, he is only in God's presence at invitation (Job)

Face-the face of God has not been seen physically by man but his "face" means His Word, His precepts and concepts, the doctrine of His Word. It means that if you focus your attention on gaining insight into Him, you become distracted from your current situation. Too many of us focus too much on the situation while we speak of being faithful, we rarely demonstrate. Seeking God's face during times of troubles strengthens you as you develop that faith muscle. By focusing on Him you remove yourself and your energy away from the problems while he works them out. You allow God to work in your life, He will. Too often we wait until the situation is so out of control then we turn to Him in desperation. God wants us to come to Him because we believe that He is true to his Word, that when Jesus stated, "Ask the Father for anything in My Name, and He will give it to you" we not only believe it we live it.

And-another conjunction which connects this first concept the concept that follows. And also that we must do the first as well as the second.

Turn-requires movement, it requires a conscious effort to take action. We can think things like I'll turn; I'm going to turn" I was thinking I should turn; I sure wish I would turn, etc, but until you actually turn, you cannot continue. Turn means that you first acknowledge that God is God; secondly you admit that your current situation is contrary to God's will in your life, and finally, you take the first step in faith. In my studies of the Bible and in my attempts to grow closer to God, I noticed how quickly most of the patriarchs of the Bible immediately acted when God told them to move. There was no hesitation, no questioning, just movement toward the goal he had set. There were no excuses as to why they couldn't fulfill the task he placed in front of them, just obedience. In order to move toward the mark of the high calling you have to turn to face the direction God has placed on your heart.

From-This is a word often used to denote direction and or specific location. Often in my travels individuals ask me "where are you from" I normally proceed to tell them where I am currently living but always include my hometown of Columbus Ohio. Or they will ask it to inquire which direction I'm going in relationship to where I have been. Whichever concept you adopt it clearly means that you are moving from one place toward another-again requires movement.

Their-denotes ownership. This is God's means to develop your individualized treatment plan. This is a plan that is used in many fields to guide the counselor/patient to reach their state goals and objectives. When I work with patients, it is imperative that we develop a plan that is something they desire and that the goals and objectives that we develop are in line with these stated desires. It also serves as a means to open dialogue when they struggle or resist the changes, I can use the plan to remind them that these were goals they desirured and they I ask them is the behavior that you have been displaying are moving you closer to or from your stated goals. Based on their answers we move to decide what action should be taken, either change the behavior or change the goals. Our walk with Jesus is similar. You either move toward Him or away from Him, if we say that we want to be Christ-like then it should be quite easy to change our behaviors because He gave us a list of what we are to be as I stated in previous paragraphs in the B-attitudes scriptures. The struggle comes from within us. I watch people struggle within their own mind with behaviors that they fully understand are detrimental to their well-being, but they continued.

Wicked-God is clear about his expectations of how we are to act, wicked is just a willingness to cause harm to others. Your motives are to hurt. We have many unresolved feelings about family members, friends, acquaintances etc. We have resentments that move us to act before we consider God's ways. You can hide these feelings in your heart of hearts from man, but you can never hide them from God. Sooner or later it will reveal itself.

Ways-Ways are often used to describe paths or courses that we take. Jesus say that I am the Way the Truth and the Life, no man can go to the Father except by me. Are your paths leading you to God? There are only two directions. To or fro-anything else you are not moving.

Then-conditional. We have to have accomplished the previous scriptures for the remainder of this passage to manifest itself in our lives. I have worked most of my life for myself. Once I left the state agencies, I never expected to receive a paycheck from them. Receiving the benefits of working for the agency was conditional on my being employed by the agency. Why do we not understand that about God? Once He gives us the requirements to receive His benefits, the only question is whether you going to do it or not; not is He true to His Word.

I-God is telling us that He will step up and move to assist us in our trials and tribulations. He himself will reach out to us in our darkness, once we have followed the prescription. We have all received prescriptions from a physician. We don't get the prescription from the doctor, take it home, lay it on the coffee table, dust it off periodically, and then complain because it didn't work. We don't talk about how the doctor doesn't know what he's doing. No, we take the prescription to the pharmacy and receive the medication and direction or how to take the medications and then we expect to see results. But we don't do that with God. This passage clearly tells us as individuals, as families, as communities, what we need to to do to heal ourselves. We just don't listen.

Will-This is a promise with purpose. God will. Not only wills He, He already has. If you will take the time to be still and look at all of the situations that you have experienced where you didn't know which way to turn or what to do, then all of a sudden "something happen" to open up an opportunity that was there and the situation is resolved. That something is God; that something is the providence of God, He already knows what you need when you need, and will supply that need. This reflection helps to build your confidence in God, and your faith grows.

Hear-As I have stated before my husband and I parented 9 children and we clearly understand the difference between listening and hearing. We spent many many hours repeating instructions that our children claimed they heard, but based on their behavior, they didn't listen. Unless you have some physical impairment, you are capable of hearing. But you have to develop the skill of listening. God wants us to be active listeners. Active listeners, listen for understanding not for debate. Have you had a conversation with someone and you can tell they are just waiting to challenge a point or comment to show where you are wrong? That is not listening.

From-indicates direction. The question is where your direction comes from? We have to understand that we have two sources of knowledge, spiritual and earthly. Both are extremely important but earthly knowledge cannot replace your relationship with God.

Heaven- In this context, this is direction from God himself. How much better could it be to gain direction from the mouth of God?

I-again, God provides clear identification and ownership of this promise. There is no mediator in this context. You have his word if you have followed his directions.

Will- Will is a word that denotes power and promise. But it also denotes a desire to do. When we say we will , we are acting on

Forgive- Again Go is speaking from his loving-kindness and grace. We read this word and use our definition for forgiveness. "I'll forgive but I won't forget". God speaks to the opposite; He says that He will remember our sins no more. When we truly repent, and CHANGE our ways and action. God no longer sees us as where we are but as He plans for us to be. It's only in our sinfulness that we become a "stench" in His nostrils.

Their- You can't own mine and I can't own yours. The old folks use to say "Every tub has to sit on it's own bottom". This is why it is fruitless for you to lesson to the message to tell me what I need to do-we each have to give an account for our actions.

Sin-Any wrongdoing is sin whether purposeful or not. We sin by word, thought or deed through acts of omission or commission.

And-This conjunction joining the previous thoughts to the following thoughts. Forgiveness brings about healing.

Heal- In all accounts of Christ performing miracles in the Bible, the accounts often use the words "made whole". This is very interesting to me because current day "healers" will often have you believe that God's healing powers are limited to just your request. Actually when God's healing takes place, wholeness takes place.. I know for myself I have been awed by the healing power of God over physical ailments but what is more amazing to me is his healing of broken relationships, families, finances, the list goes on. Holding sin in your life in any capacity separates you from healing power of God.

Their-Again, the healing that takes place is mine, what God has for me is for me. My healing needs may not look like yours but I will be healed just the same.

Land-Keeping this personal, the land may be your heart. When you truly confess your sins, repent, and turn (stop) from them, God can and will heal your heart of a multitude of problems.

XVIII

A FORMULA FOR SUCCESS

(Phillipians 4:8)

This Scripture demonstrates how we can re-direct ourselves in difficult times. At the time of the loss of my parents, it was interesting the comments often made by individuals hoping to bring some solace to the family. The things that brought peace to me was the individuals who came to the house or shared with me when I say them, the experiences and/or joy that my parents had given them. I remember one particular incident with my mother who was a nurse. I had just started school studying psychology and as with anyone with a little knowledge I was dangerous.

My mother at the time worked in a hospice for children. I decided it would be good for me to go and visit and attempt to provide psychological support to them. I walked through the facility with my mother and watched the expression on the patients faces as "Pagie" (my mother's nickname) introduced me. Her demeanor brought light to their eyes and smiles on their faces. On the other hand, I was overwhelmed by the physical conditions of these children, knowing that death was pending. I was only able to stay in the facility less than 30 minutes.

As she returned to the car, I realized that I seen this scripture in action. The interaction between my mother and her patients were based on this scriptures. She and her patients focused on the spiritual gifts not the lack of physical gifts and they were blessed with peace.

As I stated earlier, my father was a recovering alcoholic who was in recovery most of my life. I attended a funeral of one of my grandmothers' sisters. During the service I share my feelings regarding my aunt and her impact of my life. After the service two elderly gentlemen approached me and asked me was I Tom Page's daughter? I answer yes and both began to share their story of their alcoholism and the call they made to my father which changed their lives. My son was with me and to hear these stories regarding his grandfather (whom he never knew) moved to tears. They used the same words depicted in this text in describing my dad and how he encouraged them through their most difficult time.

XIX

IT'S COMING UP AGAIN

(Proverbs 21:16)

It is imperative that we understand that all that we do and say affects what we receive. There is nothing that we can hide forever, we can of course, mask or camouflage our behaviors, but the body and spirit is true to itself and will reveal the truth sooner or later. You can't run from yourself. It's just like school, you can't go to the next level until you finish the work, when you try to skip or jump over lessons, and you lose the ability to create a solid foundation for growth and may have to repeat the lesson. So when you look for the lesson and the teacher will show up to teach you. In the secular world as well as the religious world, there have been so many examples of individuals who thought they "got away" only to have their behaviors identified at later date. It the Bible says clearer' every deed done in the dark, shall come to light". There is no doubt or question in this statement. Then why don't we live according to that which we believe.

I have experienced God enough in my life to know that He is true to His Word. I had situation occur where I believed that I had "gotten away". But invariably I was exposed spiritually, emotionally or physically. But through the Grace of God, most of the exposures occurred during my awareness of Him as I began to grow to Him. I am thankful that He allowed me to learn from a gentler place than others that I have observed. But I have always attempted to move toward him when He gave me insight into behaviors or thoughts which were not acceptable to Him. I believe this comes from my understanding that God does love me as His child and what parent would hurt his child. I love all of my children and have great pride in their accomplishments and who have they become. While I am in my humanness, I love and care for them despite some of their behaviors and chooses. So if I can love them in my imperfection, I know that God loves me as His child and will bless me accordingly. He guides and supports me the manner in which I need to be supported. He teaches me in the manner I need to learn and I pray that he will continue to show this Fatherly love to me. However that does not mean that when I am wrong he will not chastise me. I share with my church family a visualization that often use when I come to the crossroads of decision making. I don't believe we make decisions based on what we know, rather more on what we want. Our society has moved from a community to "get more" attitude. In this visualization, I am standing before Christ at judgment and attempting to explain the situation to Him based on what I want, rather than what I should do. The answers become so clear, questions just fade away. We absolutely know what we should do; we just have to choose to do it. At the time of this writing I have seventeen grandchildren ranging in age from 18 months to 26 years. From a very early age they have always know what is right or wrong, what they have struggled with whether or not to do the right thing. This knowledge dulls with influences from many sources however the only way to sharpen this insight is by the Word of God and when you find His Voice, "Who Will You Need to Ask?"

GLORIA D. JONES PHD
BIOGRAPHY

So, who *was* she *"supposed"* to ask?"

Businessperson, Educator, Counselor, Wife, Mother, Grandmother, Cancer Survivor and Author, these are just a few of the accolades attributed to Gloria D. Jones, PhD. A trail of accreditations and professional designations follow her name like the many protégés she has nurtured throughout the course of both her professional career and her personal life. If at any one point in her remarkable life Dr. Jones sought the approval of outside, earthly sources to decide how she was going to live her life her accomplishments would have paled in comparison to those that she has achieved and the extraordinary woman she is today.

Dr. Gloria D. Jones was born on February 27 1954 in Columbus Ohio. The product of a middle class upbringing, her mother a nurse and her father a postman; she was no stranger to a hardworking, often tumultuous home environment. Her father was a recovering alcoholic and this was her first exposure to addiction. She would learn later in life how meaningful that exposure would become in her practice as a leading therapist in her field of substance abuse counseling.

As the second of three daughters, Dr. Jones was the typical middle child, constantly on a quest to gain her own identity, even if it meant fighting for it. Having grown up in the midst of the civil rights movement her exposure to "fighting for what was right" was further bolstered by the rising popularity of the Black Power movement in the 1960's. Her persistent journey to find herself and to question authority was under the constant scrutiny of her teachers and mentors. Her path was not to be measured by anyone else's roadmap. While her more impressionable years we challenging for her in terms of her compliance to everyone else's ideals, she thrived in academia and graduated high school a year in advance of her classmates. Gloria was well on her way to venture into the world on her own. She elected to attend a local college to pursue a degree in Physical Education. Soon she discovered that becoming a P.E. Teacher was not her calling. During this time, she met and married her first husband. The family relocated to Germany and upon the end their marriage, Gloria, now 21 years of age and with three young children, enlisted in the United States Air Force. The decision changed her life forever. First, she was stationed in Phoenix, Arizona and then Denver, Colorado. A random yet fateful encounter with a senior officer regarding balancing her busy military career and her maternal obligations evolved into a courtship, a storybook-like romance, and a subsequent 30-year marriage to her now husband, Dr. Leon Jones PhD. In all, she has given birth to three children and has parented six other children with her husband giving her nine experiences as a mother and mentor.

Gloria D. Jones is a licensed professional counselor with a PhD in Clinical Psychology from Capella University. She is a certified addiction counselor, a certified clinical supervisor in the state of Georgia and holds credentialing as a certified national addiction counselor. Dr. Jones has also obtained a Master of Arts degree from Webster College, and a B.A. in Psychology from Columbia University. Among her numerous titles is Executive Director of The Heritage Foundation Inc., Thomasville, Georgia. This highly regarded organization spawned from a community outreach program that Dr. Jones originally established to enlighten disenfranchised, primarily African-American youth about their rich cultural heritage. While working with the youth, she discovered a myriad of socio-economic and psychosocial issues that were deeply rooted in the fabric of the community. These issues were self-perpetuating, and detrimental to the youth as individuals, their family structure, and the community as a whole. In her daily role as the Executive Director of the Heritage Foundation, Inc., she is better able to directly influence change in the community through this multifaceted, non-profit organization, which was founded in 1989. Through her vision and her relentless determination to give back and to better the lives of hundreds of people, her organization has developed more than 10 treatment programs for addictive disorders, child and adolescent mental health services and prevention programs.

Throughout her career, Gloria D. Jones has written more than $6 million in grants. She continues to use both her platform and her voice to directly serve the people of her community by advocating on their behalf. Her most significant writing to date could be considered her first book aptly named, **"Who Was I Supposed to Ask…Living in God's Authority."** Through its pages, Dr. Jones shares her personal outlook and experiences in life bolstered by spiritual messages she has encountered in her walk, her devotion to and her personal relationship with GOD. She "ministers" to her readers in a way that is non-judgmental, real, insightful, and inspirational. She has been inspired by a handful of powerful women who have crossed her path in life; among them are her Aunt Juana and Maya Angelou.

Dr. Jones' most recent battle has been her diagnosis, treatment and her subsequent remission from ovarian cancer; a subject that she faces head on as she has done with all the struggles in her life. She attributes her strength to passages in the bible that both empower her and comfort her spirit. Among them, Romans, 8:28 *"And we know all things work together for good for those that love God and are called according to his purpose:"* "All things," she says, include my fight with Cancer. The writing of her book provided her with a cathartic release that allowed her to rid herself of not only physical toxins, but psycho-spiritual ones as well. The doctor had to become the patient. Throughout the experience of writing the book, she was forced to stop, adjust, and realign herself with her calling.

Now on a mission to remind everyone, through her book that faith and belief is not only real but that it works, she stands as a living, breathing testament to that philosophy. "While many people choose to look to others for human authority to step into their calling, I believe that GOD is a now GOD," she says. "He came so that we could have life and life more abundantly; not later on, or tomorrow, or next year, not even in the afterlife, but right now! That's not something you need to ask anyone's permission to have!"

CPSIA information can be obtained at www.ICGtesting.com
Printed in the USA
243836LV00002B/2/P